# Alligators Always Dress for Dinner

## An Alphabet Book of Vintage Photographs

Linda Donigan & Michael Horwitz

Images from the Past, Inc.
Bennington, Vermont

# Dedication

For Cakes and my parents L.D.
For my mother and father M.H.

# Acknowledgements

We are deeply grateful to Tordis Ilg Isselhardt for all her enthusiasm and support.
Special thanks to the following people and institutions for their generosity and assistance:

* Eugene Goldfield
* Bob Donigan
* Karen Kane
* Susan Mathews
* Andreas Brown

* Henry Deeks
* Berkshire County Historical Society
* Park-McCullough House
* Gene Kosche

1 2 3 4 5 6 7 8 9 10 XXX 03 02 01 00 99 99 98 97

Library of Congress Cataloging-in-Publication Data
Donigan, Linda, 1951-
    Alligators always dress for dinner: an alphabet book of vintage photographs/by Linda Donigan & Michael Horwitz.
    p.   cm.
    Summary: Presents each letter of the alphabet illustrated with reproductions of photographs from the late nineteenth and early twentieth centuries.
ISBN 1-884592-08-2
1. English language—Alphabet—Juvenile literature.
2. Photography—Juvenile literature.   [1. Alphabet.]   I. Horwitz, Michael, 1952-  .  II. Title.
PE1155.D66   1997
428.1—dc21
[E]                                                                                                           97-25481
                                                                                                              CIP
                                                                                                              AC

Copyright © 1997 Images from the Past, Inc.
Published by Images from the Past, Inc., Bennington, Vermont 05201
Tordis Ilg Isselhardt, Publisher

Printed in the United State of America

At your local bookstore or from Images from the Past, Inc., Box 137, Bennington, Vermont 05201     (888) 442-3204
ISBN 1-884592-08-2     $25.00

When ordering, please add $3.50 shipping and handling for the first book and $1 for each additional. 5% sales tax for shipments to Vermont. Catalog available.

*Text: Sabon • Display: SanVito • Paper: 80 lb. Dull Text • Production: hybrid Open Prepress Interface and Hand-stripping, between Stillwater Studio, Stillwater, NY and Excelsior Printing, North Adams, MA • ECRM Autokon 1030 black & white scanner • Agfa SelectSet 7000 Imagesetter with Dual Star 600 RIPs • Press: Miller TP104 with Unimatic C-3 console, six units with two perfecting cylinders 28.375 x 41 • Printer: Excelsior Printing, North Adams, MA*

# Aa

## Alligators Always Dress for Dinner

Beholding Beauty

Cc

Cornstalking

# Dd

## Dandy Driver

# Ee

## Elephantine Conga Line

Ff

Fluted Fingers

# Gg

## Goldie
## and her Bears

# Hh

## A Horn
## and a Half

# Ii

## Eyeing Ice

Jj

Juggler Brothers

Kk

Kiddie-Up

Loyal Love

Mm

Man and Machine

# Nn

## Northern Plains Nation

# Oceangoing

# PP
## Picnicking on Pie

Qq

Queen
of the Pagodas

# Rr

Rollerbears

# Ss

## Storefront Snapshot

# Tt

## Tiers of Tea Terraces

Undercover

Vv

Riverview Village

# Ww

## Working
## the Bandwagon

Xx

Exercise Guys

Yy

Yoked Yankee

# A—Z

## Aa

"From old friend Harvie and his pair of pet gators keeping warm during the winter of 1904—in Florida."

Around the turn of the 20th century, vacations became part of the lives of working people for the first time. Sunny Florida was a popular destination—trains carried hundreds of tourists south and tons of oranges north. Photo postcards, such as this funny portrait, were a new way to record these special trips. Harvie sent the card to a friend across the country in Pasadena, California.

## Bb

Beautifully dressed and adorned, this Kikuyu couple posed before the camera in the early 1900's. The Kikuyu are part of the Bantu tribe, who live in the shadow of Mt. Kenya, Africa's second highest peak. Images like this may have been an American's first glimpse of African culture. Notice his hair, which has been plaited (braided) with mud.

## Cc

Hide and seek becomes a much tougher game in a country cornfield. In seconds, you can disappear into the ears. Photo dated 1916.

# Dd

Henry Ford did not invent the automobile, but by 1908 he had developed the assembly line to produce them cheaply. His Model T sold for $350 and changed the country forever.

The dapper student driver in this photo from the early 1900's looks prepared to take his luxury touring car on the open road. Note the steering wheel on the right-hand side, common in cars of that period.

# Ee

"As long as there are clowns and elephants, there will be a circus," said P.T. Barnum, father of the modern American circus. Jumbo was the most famous elephant star of his "Greatest Show on Earth" extravaganza.

In the spectacular line-up seen here, eighteen pachyderms perform under the Big Top—but as many as 50 elephants at a time have entertained audiences since they first appeared in early 19th-century circuses.

# Ff

Perched on wooden clogs, this wandering Japanese Zen monk plays the shakuhachi, a bamboo recorder. The woven sedge (grass) hat or fukaamigasa, covers his face, and emphasizes a life devoted to contemplation.

# Gg

Our well-known version of *Goldilocks and The Three Bears* first appeared in *Mother Goose's Fairy Tales of 1878*. 35 years later, Goldilocks, in high-buttoned shoes, acts out the tale with three bear friends, possibly in a school play. Photo dated 1913.

# Hh

Props and painted backdrops were the photographer's way of creating a variety of moods to suit different sitters. Everything from picturesque landscapes and paper moons to silly scenes were popular. In this shot, Hubert balances 4-year-old friend, Gladys, on the bell of his bass horn, in front of a mysterious-looking stairway.

# Ii

Before photography, local events, celebrations and disasters were illustrated or described with words. By the end of the 19th century, they could be captured on film in precise detail.

During the frigid winter of 1887–88, a 175-foot spring-fed fountain in Bennington, Vermont turned into a mountain of ice, mimicking the tree behind. A local photographer snapped the scene—recording it for all time.

# Jj

Juggling was at its height in America when these two brothers posed with their pins. Traveling troops of entertainers crisscrossed the country, performing in small halls, theaters and opera houses. Along with song and dance acts, magicians, acrobats and jugglers brought vaudeville variety to small towns everywhere.

# Kk

On a farm, animals often do double duty—they are part of the world of work and play. Their backs are used to pull plows and playmates alike. These children from the rural South pose barefoot and bareback on one of their favorite four-footed friends.

## Ll

A good portrait captures something of the character and personality of the sitter. In a blink of the camera's eye, we get a lasting look at love.

## Mm

By the early 1900's, America's manufacturing outranked every country in the world. The importance of machines rivaled the people who operated them. But working together, as in this photo of a proud man with his drill press, they produced the cars and planes that would change the world.

## Nn

The group of tribes that make up the Sioux Nation have lived for centuries across the great northern plains of America. Sioux ceremonies such as the Sun Dance would last as long as four days—attracting thousands of Native Americans. The large summer gatherings, still held today, keep Sioux culture alive. Traditional beaded clothing and eagle-feather headdresses in this photograph create striking patterns, even when seen from behind.

## Oo

The first panoramic image was taken shortly after photography was invented in the 1840's. Special cameras with movable or wide-angle lenses captured everything from huge groups of people to sprawling vistas.

In this panoramic view of lower Manhattan, New York, the shift from sails to steam power can be seen right before our eyes.

# Pp

One can only guess what occasion prompted this picnic celebration. A graduation? With suit coats, ties and flowers in every lapel, these boys certainly were not dressed for working the fields behind them. It looks as if the picnic pie was enjoyed by the dog, as well!

# Qq

Pagodas are tower-shaped shrines built to express devotion to the Buddha. This young admirer sits among the hundreds erected in the shadow of the great Shwe Dagon Pagoda, in Burma (now Myanmar).

# Rr

The first roller skates, it is thought, were made with wooden spools by a Dutch ice skater who wanted to skate year-round. Steel ball-bearing wheels, patented in 1884, smoothed out the ride and set off a roller-skating craze that swept America—including the bears!

# Ss

Family life must have revolved around the store for these Parisian parents and their children, circa 1900. Beautifully arranged bottles, cans and brooms create a frame for this proud family of eight.

## Tt

Stereographs are two photographs mounted on one card—each taken from a slightly different angle. When viewed through a stereoscope, the scene appears three-dimensional.

   This cheerful Japanese tea picker paused on a sandy terrace long enough to be recorded for posterity. The image is one-half of a stereo card.

## Uu

Advertising was big business even when these boys posed in 1915. Their father was superintendent of the E.Z. Waist Co., a knitting factory that made the union suits they are modeling. Each box of wool-and-cotton underwear included a label with the Hall Brothers' revealing portrait.

## Vv

The beauty of a traditional African village is simple in form and function. House building in rural Africa has always been a family task, using materials close at hand—plastered sticks and grass thatch. A house is usually made up of a group of separate buildings (rooms). In some places, it's hard to know where one home stops and another begins. The village in this vintage photograph sits as many do—by a river.

## Ww

The Adam Forepaugh Circus ordered this magnificent Lion and Mirror Bandwagon built in 1879. After 11 years, it was acquired by Ringling Brothers for use in their first railroad circus. The Cole Brothers Circus Band (seen here) was next to play atop the wagon as it rolled across America entertaining audiences well into the 20th century. Note: the mirrors have been replaced by crossed swords.

# Xx

The sport of gymnastics came to America from Europe with the great wave of immigrants at the end of the 19th and beginning of the 20th century. Clubs formed where gymnasts, like these enthusiasts of the Swiss Gymnastics Society, were referred to as "turners."

# Yy

Coming home from school and picking potatoes? A little harvesting before church? There must be some reason this New England boy has a tie on underneath his overalls.

# Zz

Sometimes a photograph is interesting just because of its textures or patterns. In this slice-of-life image, the plaid coats of two Scottish schoolgirls vibrate against the diamond fence and zebra stripes.

# Photo Credits